50 Scottish Recipes for Home

By: Kelly Johnson

Table of Contents

- Haggis
- Scottish Shortbread
- Scotch Broth
- Cranachan
- Cullen Skink
- Cock-a-Leekie Soup
- Neeps and Tatties
- Dundee Cake
- Scottish Oatcakes
- Arbroath Smokies
- Forfar Bridies
- Selkirk Bannock
- Rumbledethumps
- Scotch Eggs
- Stovies
- Tattie Scones
- Black Bun
- Mince and Tatties
- Scotch Pancakes
- Kedgeree
- Tablet
- Clootie Dumpling
- Partan Bree
- Finnan Haddie
- Smoked Salmon with Whisky Sauce
- Bannock
- Stornoway Black Pudding
- Leek and Potato Soup
- Highland Beef Stew
- Cranberry and Orange Scones
- Skirlie
- Scottish Oatcakes
- Rumbledethumps
- Stuffed Sheep's Stomach (a variation of haggis)
- Scones with Clotted Cream and Jam

- Scottish Salmon Pie
- Scottish Salmon Fillets with Lemon and Dill
- Vegetarian Haggis
- Venison Pie
- Scotch Lamb Hotpot
- Scotch Whisky Trifle
- Scottish Steak Pie
- Potato and Leek Soup
- Smoked Mackerel Pate
- Clapshot
- Scotch Beef Wellington
- Scottish Cheese Platter
- Scottish Gin and Tonic Cake
- Scottish Ale and Beef Stew
- Scottish Butter Tablet

Haggis

Ingredients:

- 1 sheep's pluck (heart, liver, and lungs)
- 1 sheep's stomach
- 3 cups finely chopped suet
- 1 large onion, finely chopped
- 3 cups steel-cut oats
- 2 cups beef stock
- 1 teaspoon salt
- 1 teaspoon black pepper
- 1 teaspoon ground coriander
- 1 teaspoon nutmeg
- 1 teaspoon allspice

Instructions:

1. Rinse the sheep's stomach thoroughly under cold running water and soak it in cold salted water overnight. This helps to clean and soften it.
2. In a large pot of lightly salted water, boil the sheep's pluck (heart, liver, and lungs) for about 2 hours or until tender. Remove and allow to cool.
3. Once cooled, finely chop the cooked pluck, removing any excess fat or gristle.
4. In a large mixing bowl, combine the chopped pluck, suet, chopped onion, and oats. Mix well.
5. Season the mixture with salt, pepper, coriander, nutmeg, and allspice. Mix until well combined.
6. Stuff the mixture into the cleaned sheep's stomach, filling it about two-thirds full. Be sure to leave some room for the mixture to expand during cooking.
7. Sew up the stomach securely with a needle and thread, ensuring there are no gaps or openings.
8. Place the haggis in a large pot and add enough beef stock to cover it completely.
9. Bring the stock to a gentle simmer, then reduce the heat and cover the pot with a lid.
10. Allow the haggis to simmer gently for about 3 hours, or until cooked through and piping hot.
11. Once cooked, carefully remove the haggis from the pot and transfer it to a serving platter.

12. To serve, cut open the haggis with a sharp knife and spoon out the filling onto serving plates.

Traditionally, haggis is served with neeps (mashed turnips) and tatties (mashed potatoes), along with a drizzle of whisky sauce. Enjoy your homemade haggis!

Scottish Shortbread

Ingredients:

- 1 cup (2 sticks) unsalted butter, softened
- 1/2 cup granulated sugar
- 2 cups all-purpose flour
- 1/4 teaspoon salt
- Extra granulated sugar, for sprinkling (optional)

Instructions:

1. Preheat your oven to 325°F (160°C). Prepare a baking sheet by lining it with parchment paper.
2. In a large mixing bowl, cream together the softened butter and granulated sugar until light and fluffy.
3. Sift the flour and salt into the creamed butter and sugar mixture. Mix until a dough forms. You can also use a wooden spoon or your hands to mix the dough.
4. Transfer the dough onto a lightly floured surface. Knead it gently until it comes together and becomes smooth.
5. Roll out the dough to about 1/2 inch (1.25 cm) thickness. You can shape it into a rectangle or circle, depending on your preference.
6. Use a sharp knife or a cookie cutter to cut the dough into desired shapes. Traditional shapes include rectangles, squares, or rounds.
7. Place the shortbread shapes onto the prepared baking sheet, leaving some space between each piece.
8. If desired, prick each shortbread piece with a fork to create a decorative pattern.
9. Optionally, sprinkle some granulated sugar over the tops of the shortbread pieces for extra sweetness and crunch.
10. Place the baking sheet in the preheated oven and bake the shortbread for 20-25 minutes, or until lightly golden around the edges.
11. Once baked, remove the shortbread from the oven and allow it to cool on the baking sheet for a few minutes.
12. Transfer the shortbread to a wire rack to cool completely before serving.

Scottish shortbread is delicious served alongside a cup of tea or coffee. Store any leftovers in an airtight container at room temperature for up to one week. Enjoy your homemade Scottish shortbread!

Scotch Broth

Ingredients:

- 1 lb (450g) lamb neck or shoulder, bone-in
- 1 onion, chopped
- 2 carrots, peeled and diced
- 2 stalks celery, diced
- 1 leek, sliced
- 2 cloves garlic, minced
- 1/2 cup pearl barley
- 6 cups beef or vegetable broth
- 2 bay leaves
- 2 sprigs fresh thyme (or 1 teaspoon dried thyme)
- Salt and pepper, to taste
- Chopped fresh parsley, for garnish (optional)

Instructions:

1. In a large soup pot or Dutch oven, heat a little oil over medium heat. Add the lamb pieces and brown them on all sides, about 5 minutes. Remove the lamb from the pot and set aside.
2. In the same pot, add the chopped onion, carrots, celery, leek, and garlic. Sauté until the vegetables are softened, about 5-7 minutes.
3. Return the browned lamb to the pot. Add the pearl barley, beef or vegetable broth, bay leaves, and thyme to the pot. Season with salt and pepper to taste.
4. Bring the broth to a boil, then reduce the heat to low. Cover the pot and let the soup simmer gently for about 1 to 1 1/2 hours, or until the lamb is tender and the barley is cooked.
5. Once the lamb is tender, remove it from the pot and let it cool slightly. Remove the meat from the bones and shred it into bite-sized pieces. Discard any bones and excess fat.
6. Return the shredded lamb meat to the pot. Taste the soup and adjust the seasoning if necessary.
7. Serve the Scotch Broth hot, garnished with chopped fresh parsley if desired.

Scotch Broth is hearty and comforting, perfect for a chilly day. Enjoy it with some crusty bread or oatcakes on the side.

Cranachan

Ingredients:

- 1 cup (240ml) heavy cream
- 2 tablespoons honey
- 1/4 cup (25g) rolled oats
- 2 tablespoons whisky (such as Scotch whisky)
- 2 cups (200g) fresh raspberries
- Extra raspberries, for garnish (optional)

Instructions:

1. In a small skillet, toast the rolled oats over medium heat until golden brown and fragrant, about 5 minutes. Stir constantly to prevent burning. Remove from heat and let cool.
2. In a mixing bowl, whip the heavy cream until stiff peaks form.
3. Gently fold the honey and whisky into the whipped cream until well combined.
4. Reserve a few raspberries for garnish, then gently fold the remaining raspberries into the whipped cream mixture.
5. To assemble the Cranachan, spoon alternating layers of the whipped cream mixture and toasted oats into serving glasses or bowls.
6. Top each serving with a few reserved raspberries for garnish.
7. Serve the Cranachan immediately, or refrigerate until ready to serve.

Cranachan is best enjoyed fresh, but you can refrigerate it for up to several hours before serving. It's a delightful dessert with a perfect balance of sweetness, creaminess, and a hint of whisky flavor. Enjoy!

Cullen Skink

Ingredients:

- 1 lb (450g) smoked haddock fillets, skin-on
- 2 tablespoons unsalted butter
- 1 onion, finely chopped
- 2 medium potatoes, peeled and diced
- 2 cups (480ml) fish or vegetable stock
- 1 cup (240ml) whole milk
- 1 cup (240ml) heavy cream
- Salt and pepper, to taste
- Chopped fresh parsley, for garnish (optional)

Instructions:

1. In a large pot, melt the butter over medium heat. Add the chopped onion and sauté until softened, about 5 minutes.
2. Add the diced potatoes to the pot and stir to coat them in the butter and onions.
3. Pour in the fish or vegetable stock and bring the mixture to a simmer. Cook for about 10-15 minutes, or until the potatoes are tender.
4. While the potatoes are cooking, place the smoked haddock fillets in a separate pan and cover them with cold water. Bring the water to a gentle simmer and poach the fish for about 5 minutes, or until it is cooked through and flakes easily with a fork.
5. Once cooked, remove the haddock from the poaching liquid and carefully peel off the skin. Flake the fish into bite-sized pieces, removing any bones.
6. Add the flaked haddock, along with any juices, to the pot with the potatoes and stock.
7. Pour in the whole milk and heavy cream, stirring gently to combine. Season with salt and pepper to taste.
8. Allow the soup to simmer gently for another 5 minutes to heat through and allow the flavors to meld together.
9. Taste the soup and adjust the seasoning if necessary.
10. Serve the Cullen Skink hot, garnished with chopped fresh parsley if desired.

Cullen Skink is wonderfully comforting and perfect for a cold day. Enjoy it with some crusty bread or oatcakes on the side.

Cock-a-Leekie Soup

Ingredients:

- 2 tablespoons unsalted butter
- 1 lb (450g) boneless, skinless chicken thighs or breasts, diced
- 2 leeks, white and light green parts only, thinly sliced
- 2 carrots, peeled and diced
- 2 celery stalks, diced
- 6 cups (1.5 liters) chicken broth
- 1/2 cup (75g) pitted prunes, chopped
- 1/4 cup (50g) pearl barley (optional)
- Salt and pepper, to taste
- Chopped fresh parsley, for garnish (optional)

Instructions:

1. In a large pot or Dutch oven, melt the butter over medium heat. Add the diced chicken and cook until browned on all sides, about 5-7 minutes. Remove the chicken from the pot and set aside.
2. Add the sliced leeks, diced carrots, and diced celery to the pot. Cook, stirring occasionally, until the vegetables are softened, about 5 minutes.
3. Return the browned chicken to the pot. Pour in the chicken broth and bring the mixture to a simmer.
4. If using, add the pearl barley to the pot. Simmer the soup, partially covered, for about 30 minutes, or until the barley is tender.
5. Stir in the chopped prunes and continue to simmer for another 5-10 minutes, until the prunes are softened and the flavors are well combined.
6. Taste the soup and season with salt and pepper to taste.
7. Ladle the Cock-a-Leekie Soup into serving bowls and garnish with chopped fresh parsley if desired.

Cock-a-Leekie Soup is hearty and flavorful, perfect for a cold day. Serve it with some crusty bread or Scottish oatcakes on the side for a complete meal. Enjoy!

Neeps and Tatties

Ingredients:

- 2 large turnips (swedes), peeled and diced
- 2 tablespoons butter
- Salt and pepper, to taste
- Optional: a pinch of nutmeg or a drizzle of honey (for extra flavor)

Instructions:

1. Place the diced turnips in a large pot and cover them with water. Add a pinch of salt to the water.
2. Bring the water to a boil over medium-high heat, then reduce the heat to low and simmer the turnips until they are tender, about 20-25 minutes.
3. Once the turnips are tender, drain them well and return them to the pot.
4. Add the butter to the pot and mash the turnips with a potato masher or fork until smooth. You can also use a hand blender for a smoother consistency.
5. Season the mashed turnips with salt and pepper to taste. If desired, add a pinch of nutmeg or a drizzle of honey for extra flavor.
6. Serve the neeps hot as a delicious side dish.

Tatties (Mashed Potatoes):

Ingredients:

- 2 lbs (about 1 kg) potatoes, peeled and diced
- 4 tablespoons butter
- 1/2 cup (120ml) milk or cream
- Salt and pepper, to taste
- Optional: chopped fresh parsley or chives for garnish

Instructions:

1. Place the diced potatoes in a large pot and cover them with cold water. Add a pinch of salt to the water.

2. Bring the water to a boil over medium-high heat, then reduce the heat to low and simmer the potatoes until they are tender, about 15-20 minutes.
3. Once the potatoes are tender, drain them well and return them to the pot.
4. Add the butter and milk (or cream) to the pot with the potatoes.
5. Mash the potatoes with a potato masher or fork until smooth and creamy. You can also use a hand mixer for a smoother texture.
6. Season the mashed potatoes with salt and pepper to taste. If desired, garnish with chopped fresh parsley or chives.
7. Serve the tatties hot as a comforting side dish.

Enjoy your neeps and tatties alongside your favorite Scottish meal!

Dundee Cake

Ingredients:

- 1 1/2 cups (225g) all-purpose flour
- 1/2 teaspoon baking powder
- 1/4 teaspoon salt
- 3/4 cup (170g) unsalted butter, softened
- 3/4 cup (150g) granulated sugar
- 3 large eggs
- 1 tablespoon orange zest
- 1 tablespoon lemon zest
- 1/4 cup (60ml) orange juice
- 1/4 cup (60ml) lemon juice
- 1 cup (150g) currants
- 1 cup (150g) sultanas (golden raisins)
- 1/2 cup (75g) chopped candied peel (optional)
- 1/2 cup (75g) blanched almonds, roughly chopped
- Whole blanched almonds, for decoration
- 2 tablespoons apricot jam, for glazing

Instructions:

1. Preheat your oven to 325°F (160°C). Grease a 9-inch (23cm) round cake tin and line the bottom with parchment paper.
2. In a medium bowl, sift together the flour, baking powder, and salt. Set aside.
3. In a large mixing bowl, cream together the softened butter and granulated sugar until light and fluffy.
4. Beat in the eggs, one at a time, until well combined. Add the orange zest and lemon zest, and mix until incorporated.
5. Gradually add the flour mixture to the wet ingredients, alternating with the orange juice and lemon juice, until a smooth batter forms.
6. Fold in the currants, sultanas, chopped candied peel (if using), and chopped almonds until evenly distributed throughout the batter.
7. Pour the batter into the prepared cake tin and smooth the top with a spatula. Arrange whole blanched almonds on top of the cake in a decorative pattern.
8. Bake the Dundee Cake in the preheated oven for 60-70 minutes, or until golden brown and a skewer inserted into the center comes out clean.

9. Remove the cake from the oven and allow it to cool in the tin for 10 minutes. Then, carefully transfer the cake to a wire rack to cool completely.
10. Once the cake has cooled, warm the apricot jam in a small saucepan over low heat until it becomes liquid. Brush the top of the cake with the warm apricot jam to glaze.
11. Allow the glaze to set before serving the Dundee Cake. Slice and enjoy with a cup of tea or coffee.

Dundee Cake is a deliciously moist and fruity cake that is perfect for any occasion. It can be stored in an airtight container for several days.

Scottish Oatcakes

Ingredients:

- 1 cup (90g) rolled oats (not instant)
- 1/2 cup (60g) oat flour (you can make your own by grinding oats in a food processor)
- 1/4 teaspoon baking powder
- 1/2 teaspoon salt
- 2 tablespoons unsalted butter, melted
- Approximately 1/4 cup (60ml) warm water

Instructions:

1. Preheat your oven to 350°F (175°C). Line a baking sheet with parchment paper.
2. In a mixing bowl, combine the rolled oats, oat flour, baking powder, and salt.
3. Add the melted butter to the dry ingredients and mix until well combined.
4. Gradually add the warm water, a little at a time, stirring until a thick dough forms. You may not need to use all of the water; stop adding water once the dough comes together.
5. Turn the dough out onto a lightly floured surface and knead it gently until smooth.
6. Roll out the dough to a thickness of about 1/8 inch (3mm). Use a cookie cutter or a knife to cut the dough into rounds or shapes of your choice.
7. Transfer the oatcakes to the prepared baking sheet and prick them all over with a fork to prevent them from puffing up during baking.
8. Bake the oatcakes in the preheated oven for 15-20 minutes, or until they are lightly golden and firm to the touch.
9. Remove the oatcakes from the oven and transfer them to a wire rack to cool completely.
10. Once cooled, store the oatcakes in an airtight container at room temperature for up to one week.

Scottish oatcakes are delicious served plain or topped with cheese, butter, jam, or your favorite spread. They make a wonderful snack or addition to a cheese board. Enjoy!

Arbroath Smokies

Ingredients:

- Whole fresh haddock fish, gutted and cleaned (about 1-2 per person)
- Coarse sea salt
- Hardwood chips or sawdust (such as oak or beech)

Instructions:

1. Start by preparing your smoker. You can use a traditional smoker, a stovetop smoker, or even a barbecue grill with a smoker box. The key is to use indirect heat and low, steady smoke.
2. Rinse the haddock fish under cold running water and pat them dry with paper towels.
3. Generously sprinkle coarse sea salt inside and outside of each fish, rubbing it in to ensure even seasoning. Let the fish sit at room temperature for about 30 minutes to allow the salt to penetrate.
4. If using a stovetop smoker or barbecue grill, prepare it for smoking according to the manufacturer's instructions. If using a traditional smoker, preheat it to around 180-200°F (82-93°C).
5. Once the smoker is ready, place the haddock fish directly on the grate or on a wire rack inside the smoker.
6. Add the hardwood chips or sawdust to the smoker box or directly onto the coals, depending on your setup. The smoke should be thin and steady, not billowing.
7. Smoke the haddock fish for about 30-45 minutes, or until they are cooked through and have absorbed the smoky flavor. The flesh should be opaque and flake easily with a fork.
8. Remove the smoked haddock from the smoker and let them cool slightly before serving.

Traditionally, Arbroath Smokies are served hot, often simply flaked and served with buttered bread or potatoes. They can also be used in various dishes, such as fish pies or chowders. Enjoy your homemade Arbroath Smokies!

Forfar Bridies

Ingredients:

For the pastry:

- 2 cups (250g) all-purpose flour
- 1/2 cup (115g) unsalted butter, cold and cubed
- Pinch of salt
- 1/4 cup (60ml) cold water

For the filling:

- 1 lb (450g) lean minced beef
- 1 onion, finely chopped
- 1 medium potato, peeled and finely diced (optional)
- 1 tablespoon Worcestershire sauce
- Salt and pepper to taste
- 1 tablespoon beef dripping or vegetable oil
- 1 tablespoon flour (for thickening)

For assembly:

- 1 egg, beaten (for egg wash)

Instructions:

1. Prepare the pastry:
    - In a large bowl, combine the flour and salt. Add the cold, cubed butter.
    - Rub the butter into the flour using your fingertips until the mixture resembles breadcrumbs.
    - Gradually add the cold water, mixing until the dough comes together.
    - Shape the dough into a ball, wrap it in plastic wrap, and refrigerate for at least 30 minutes.
2. Prepare the filling:
    - In a skillet, heat the beef dripping or vegetable oil over medium heat. Add the chopped onions and sauté until translucent.

- Add the minced beef to the skillet and cook until browned, breaking it up with a spoon as it cooks.
- If using, add the diced potatoes to the skillet and cook until tender.
- Stir in the Worcestershire sauce and season with salt and pepper to taste.
- Sprinkle the flour over the filling mixture and stir well to combine. Cook for a few more minutes until thickened. Remove from heat and let cool.

3. Assemble the Forfar Bridies:
    - Preheat your oven to 375°F (190°C). Line a baking sheet with parchment paper.
    - On a lightly floured surface, roll out the chilled pastry dough to about 1/8 inch (3mm) thickness. Cut the dough into circles, about 6-8 inches (15-20cm) in diameter.
    - Spoon some of the cooled filling onto one half of each pastry circle, leaving a border around the edges.
    - Fold the other half of the pastry over the filling to enclose it, forming a semi-circle. Press the edges together to seal, then crimp with a fork to create a decorative edge.
    - Place the assembled bridies on the prepared baking sheet. Brush the tops with beaten egg for a golden finish.

4. Bake the Forfar Bridies:
    - Bake in the preheated oven for 25-30 minutes, or until the pastry is golden brown and crisp.
    - Remove from the oven and let cool slightly before serving.

Forfar Bridies are delicious served warm or at room temperature, making them a perfect snack or meal on the go. Enjoy your homemade Forfar Bridies!

Selkirk Bannock

Ingredients:

- 2 1/2 cups (300g) all-purpose flour
- 1/2 teaspoon salt
- 1 teaspoon ground cinnamon
- 1/2 teaspoon ground nutmeg
- 1/4 teaspoon ground allspice
- 1/4 teaspoon ground cloves
- 1/4 cup (50g) granulated sugar
- 1/4 cup (50g) light brown sugar
- 1/2 cup (115g) unsalted butter, cold and cubed
- 1/2 cup (75g) currants
- 1/2 cup (75g) raisins
- 1/4 cup (60ml) milk
- 2 teaspoons active dry yeast
- 1/4 cup (60ml) warm water
- 1 large egg, beaten (for egg wash)
- Demerara sugar, for sprinkling (optional)

Instructions:

1. Activate the yeast: In a small bowl, dissolve the yeast in warm water. Let it sit for about 5-10 minutes, or until frothy.
2. Prepare the dough: In a large mixing bowl, combine the flour, salt, ground cinnamon, nutmeg, allspice, cloves, granulated sugar, and light brown sugar. Mix well to combine.
3. Add the cold, cubed butter to the dry ingredients. Use your fingertips to rub the butter into the flour mixture until it resembles coarse breadcrumbs.
4. Stir in the currants and raisins until evenly distributed.
5. Make a well in the center of the flour mixture and pour in the activated yeast mixture and milk. Use a wooden spoon or your hands to mix until a dough forms.
6. Turn the dough out onto a lightly floured surface and knead it for about 5-7 minutes, or until smooth and elastic.
7. Place the dough in a greased bowl, cover with a clean kitchen towel or plastic wrap, and let it rise in a warm, draft-free place for about 1-2 hours, or until doubled in size.

8. Shape and bake the bannock: Once the dough has risen, punch it down and transfer it to a lightly floured surface.
9. Shape the dough into a round loaf and place it on a parchment-lined baking sheet. Cover loosely with a clean kitchen towel and let it rise for another 30-45 minutes.
10. Preheat your oven to 375°F (190°C).
11. Brush the risen bannock with beaten egg for a shiny finish. Optionally, sprinkle the top with Demerara sugar for added sweetness and crunch.
12. Bake the bannock in the preheated oven for 25-30 minutes, or until golden brown and hollow-sounding when tapped on the bottom.
13. Remove the bannock from the oven and let it cool on a wire rack before slicing and serving.

Selkirk Bannock is delicious served sliced and spread with butter, jam, or enjoyed on its own with a cup of tea or coffee. Enjoy your homemade Selkirk Bannock!

Rumbledethumps

Ingredients:

- 2 lbs (about 900g) potatoes, peeled and chopped into chunks
- 1 small head of cabbage, shredded
- 1 large onion, finely chopped
- 2 tablespoons butter
- 1 cup (about 100g) grated Scottish cheddar cheese (or any sharp cheddar)
- Salt and pepper, to taste
- Optional: chopped chives or parsley for garnish

Instructions:

1. Preheat your oven to 375°F (190°C). Grease a baking dish with butter or cooking spray.
2. Place the chopped potatoes in a large pot and cover them with cold water. Bring the water to a boil over medium-high heat, then reduce the heat to medium and simmer the potatoes until they are tender, about 15-20 minutes.
3. While the potatoes are cooking, bring another pot of salted water to a boil. Add the shredded cabbage to the pot and cook for about 5-7 minutes, or until the cabbage is tender. Drain well and set aside.
4. In a skillet, melt the butter over medium heat. Add the chopped onion and sauté until softened and translucent, about 5 minutes. Remove from heat and set aside.
5. Once the potatoes are cooked, drain them well and return them to the pot. Mash the potatoes until smooth and creamy.
6. Add the cooked cabbage, sautéed onions, and grated cheese to the mashed potatoes. Season with salt and pepper to taste. Stir well to combine.
7. Transfer the potato mixture to the prepared baking dish, spreading it out evenly.
8. Bake in the preheated oven for 25-30 minutes, or until the top is golden brown and bubbly.
9. Remove from the oven and let it cool slightly before serving.
10. Optionally, garnish with chopped chives or parsley before serving.

Rumbledethumps is a delicious and comforting dish that can be served as a side or even as a main course with some crusty bread on the side. Enjoy your homemade Rumbledethumps!

Scotch Eggs

Ingredients:

- 6 large eggs
- 1 lb (450g) sausage meat (pork sausage meat works well)
- 1/2 cup (60g) all-purpose flour
- 1 cup (100g) breadcrumbs
- 1 teaspoon dried herbs (such as thyme, parsley, or sage)
- Salt and pepper, to taste
- Vegetable oil, for frying

Instructions:

1. Boil the eggs: Place the eggs in a saucepan and cover them with cold water. Bring the water to a boil over medium-high heat. Once boiling, reduce the heat slightly and let the eggs simmer for 9-10 minutes. Remove from heat and transfer the eggs to a bowl of ice water to cool completely. Once cooled, peel the eggs and set aside.
2. Prepare the sausage meat: In a mixing bowl, combine the sausage meat with the dried herbs, salt, and pepper. Mix until well combined.
3. Assemble the Scotch eggs: Divide the sausage meat into 6 equal portions. Flatten each portion into a thin patty in the palm of your hand. Place a peeled hard-boiled egg in the center of each patty and gently mold the sausage meat around the egg, ensuring it is evenly covered.
4. Coat the Scotch eggs: Set up three shallow bowls: one with flour, one with beaten eggs, and one with breadcrumbs. Roll each sausage-coated egg in the flour, then dip it into the beaten egg, and finally coat it thoroughly with breadcrumbs, pressing gently to adhere.
5. Fry the Scotch eggs: Heat vegetable oil in a deep fryer or large, deep skillet to 350°F (180°C). Carefully lower the coated eggs into the hot oil, a few at a time, and fry for about 4-5 minutes, or until golden brown and crispy. Remove from the oil using a slotted spoon and transfer to a plate lined with paper towels to drain excess oil.
6. Serve: Allow the Scotch eggs to cool slightly before serving. They can be enjoyed warm or at room temperature. Cut them in half to reveal the delicious, golden crust and the perfectly cooked egg inside.

Scotch eggs are often served with dipping sauces such as mustard or aioli. They're great as a snack, appetizer, or as part of a picnic spread. Enjoy your homemade Scotch eggs!

Stovies

Ingredients:

- 4 large potatoes, peeled and thinly sliced
- 2 onions, thinly sliced
- 1 tablespoon vegetable oil or beef dripping
- 1 cup leftover cooked meat, diced (optional)
- Salt and pepper, to taste
- Beef or vegetable stock, as needed
- Chopped parsley, for garnish (optional)

Instructions:

1. Heat the vegetable oil or beef dripping in a large, heavy-bottomed pot over medium heat.
2. Add the thinly sliced onions to the pot and cook, stirring occasionally, until they are soft and golden brown, about 10-15 minutes.
3. If using leftover cooked meat, add it to the pot with the onions and cook for a few minutes to heat through.
4. Add the thinly sliced potatoes to the pot, arranging them in layers on top of the onions and meat.
5. Season the potatoes with salt and pepper to taste.
6. Pour enough beef or vegetable stock into the pot to just cover the potatoes. The stock will help to cook the potatoes and create a flavorful gravy.
7. Bring the mixture to a simmer, then reduce the heat to low and cover the pot with a lid.
8. Let the stovies simmer gently for about 30-40 minutes, or until the potatoes are tender and cooked through. Stir occasionally to prevent sticking and to help the flavors meld together.
9. Once the potatoes are cooked, use a fork or potato masher to lightly mash them in the pot. This will help to thicken the gravy and create a creamy texture.
10. Taste the stovies and adjust the seasoning if necessary.
11. Serve the stovies hot, garnished with chopped parsley if desired. They're delicious on their own or served with crusty bread or oatcakes on the side.

Stovies are a simple and comforting dish that's perfect for a cozy meal on a cold day. Feel free to customize the recipe with your favorite ingredients and seasonings. Enjoy your homemade stovies!

Tattie Scones

Ingredients:

- 2 cups (about 300g) mashed potatoes (without added milk or butter)
- 1 cup (about 125g) all-purpose flour, plus extra for dusting
- 2 tablespoons unsalted butter, melted
- Salt, to taste
- Vegetable oil or butter, for frying

Instructions:

1. In a large mixing bowl, combine the mashed potatoes, flour, melted butter, and a pinch of salt. Mix until the ingredients come together to form a soft dough. Add a little more flour if the dough is too sticky.
2. Turn the dough out onto a lightly floured surface and knead it gently for a minute or two until smooth.
3. Divide the dough into several equal-sized portions, depending on how large you want your tattie scones to be. Roll each portion into a ball.
4. On a floured surface, use a rolling pin to roll out each dough ball into a thin circle, about 1/4 inch (6mm) thick. If needed, dust the dough with a little more flour to prevent sticking.
5. Heat a little vegetable oil or butter in a large skillet or griddle over medium heat.
6. Carefully transfer the rolled-out dough circles to the hot skillet, one at a time. Cook for 2-3 minutes on each side, or until golden brown and cooked through. You may need to adjust the heat to prevent burning.
7. Remove the cooked tattie scones from the skillet and place them on a plate lined with paper towels to absorb any excess oil.
8. Repeat the process with the remaining dough portions, adding more oil or butter to the skillet as needed.
9. Once all the tattie scones are cooked, serve them warm. They're delicious on their own or served with butter, cheese, or your favorite topping.

Tattie scones are best enjoyed fresh and warm, but you can also store any leftovers in an airtight container in the refrigerator for a couple of days. Simply reheat them in a skillet or microwave before serving. Enjoy your homemade tattie scones as part of a delicious Scottish breakfast or as a tasty snack!

Black Bun

Ingredients:

For the pastry:

- 2 1/2 cups (300g) all-purpose flour
- 1/2 cup (115g) unsalted butter, cold and cubed
- Pinch of salt
- 1/4 cup (60ml) cold water

For the filling:

- 1 1/2 cups (225g) raisins
- 1 1/2 cups (225g) currants
- 1 1/2 cups (225g) chopped dates
- 1/2 cup (75g) chopped candied peel
- 1/2 cup (75g) blanched almonds, roughly chopped
- 1/2 cup (75g) ground almonds
- 1/2 cup (75g) fine breadcrumbs
- 1/2 cup (75g) dark brown sugar
- 2 teaspoons ground cinnamon
- 1 teaspoon ground ginger
- 1/2 teaspoon ground cloves
- 1/2 teaspoon ground nutmeg
- Zest of 1 lemon
- Zest of 1 orange
- 1/2 cup (120ml) whisky or brandy

For assembling:

- 1 beaten egg, for egg wash
- Demerara sugar, for sprinkling

Instructions:

1. Prepare the fruit filling: In a large mixing bowl, combine the raisins, currants, chopped dates, chopped candied peel, blanched almonds, ground almonds, breadcrumbs, dark brown sugar, ground cinnamon, ground ginger, ground cloves, ground nutmeg, lemon zest, and orange zest. Mix well to combine. Pour the

whisky or brandy over the mixture and stir until everything is evenly moistened. Cover the bowl with plastic wrap and let it sit overnight to allow the flavors to meld.
2. Make the pastry: In a large mixing bowl, combine the flour, salt, and cold, cubed butter. Use your fingertips to rub the butter into the flour until the mixture resembles coarse breadcrumbs. Gradually add the cold water, mixing until a dough forms. Shape the dough into a ball, wrap it in plastic wrap, and refrigerate for at least 30 minutes.
3. Preheat your oven to 350°F (175°C). Grease a deep 8-inch (20cm) round cake tin and line the bottom with parchment paper.
4. Assemble the Black Bun: Divide the pastry dough into two equal portions. Roll out one portion on a lightly floured surface to about 1/4 inch (6mm) thickness. Use the rolled-out pastry to line the bottom and sides of the prepared cake tin.
5. Spoon the fruit filling into the pastry-lined tin, pressing it down gently to compact it.
6. Roll out the remaining portion of pastry to about 1/4 inch (6mm) thickness. Use it to cover the top of the fruit filling, sealing the edges with the bottom pastry. Use a knife to make a few slits in the top pastry to allow steam to escape during baking.
7. Brush the top of the Black Bun with beaten egg and sprinkle with Demerara sugar.
8. Bake the Black Bun: Place the cake tin in the preheated oven and bake for 1 1/2 to 2 hours, or until the pastry is golden brown and the filling is cooked through. If the pastry begins to brown too quickly, cover it loosely with aluminum foil.
9. Cool and store: Remove the Black Bun from the oven and let it cool in the tin for about 10 minutes before transferring it to a wire rack to cool completely. Once cooled, wrap the Black Bun tightly in aluminum foil and store it in a cool, dry place for at least a week before slicing and serving. This allows the flavors to develop and mature.
10. Serve: To serve, slice the Black Bun into thin slices and enjoy with a cup of tea or coffee.

Black Bun is a delightful and festive treat that's perfect for celebrating special occasions. Enjoy making and sharing this traditional Scottish delicacy with friends and family!

Mince and Tatties

Ingredients:

For the mince:

- 1 lb (450g) lean minced beef (ground beef)
- 1 onion, finely chopped
- 2 cloves garlic, minced
- 1 carrot, finely diced (optional)
- 1 tablespoon tomato paste
- 1 cup (240ml) beef or vegetable stock
- 1 teaspoon Worcestershire sauce (optional)
- Salt and pepper, to taste
- 1 tablespoon vegetable oil

For the mashed potatoes (tatties):

- 2 lbs (about 1 kg) potatoes, peeled and chopped into chunks
- 4 tablespoons butter
- 1/2 cup (120ml) milk or cream
- Salt and pepper, to taste

Instructions:

1. Prepare the mashed potatoes (tatties):
    - Place the chopped potatoes in a large pot and cover them with cold water. Add a pinch of salt to the water.
    - Bring the water to a boil over medium-high heat, then reduce the heat to medium-low and simmer the potatoes until they are tender, about 15-20 minutes.
    - Once the potatoes are cooked, drain them well and return them to the pot.
    - Add the butter and milk (or cream) to the pot with the potatoes.
    - Mash the potatoes with a potato masher or fork until smooth and creamy. You can also use a hand mixer for a smoother texture. Season with salt and pepper to taste. Keep warm until ready to serve.
2. Prepare the mince:

- Heat the vegetable oil in a large skillet or frying pan over medium heat.
- Add the chopped onion and minced garlic to the skillet and cook, stirring occasionally, until softened and translucent, about 5 minutes.
- Add the minced beef to the skillet and cook until browned, breaking it up with a spoon as it cooks.
- If using, add the finely diced carrot to the skillet and cook until softened.
- Stir in the tomato paste, beef or vegetable stock, and Worcestershire sauce (if using). Season with salt and pepper to taste. Simmer the mixture for about 10-15 minutes, or until the sauce has thickened slightly and the flavors have melded together.

3. Serve:
    - To serve, spoon the mashed potatoes onto serving plates or bowls.
    - Top the mashed potatoes with the cooked minced beef mixture.
    - Garnish with chopped fresh parsley or chives, if desired.
    - Serve the mince and tatties hot, with additional vegetables or condiments on the side if desired.

Mince and tatties are a comforting and hearty dish that's perfect for a cozy meal on a cold day. Enjoy your homemade mince and tatties!

Scotch Pancakes

Ingredients:

- 1 cup (125g) all-purpose flour
- 1 teaspoon baking powder
- 1 tablespoon granulated sugar
- Pinch of salt
- 1 large egg
- 3/4 cup (180ml) milk
- Butter or oil, for greasing the pan

Instructions:

1. In a mixing bowl, sift together the flour, baking powder, sugar, and salt. This helps to ensure that there are no lumps in the batter.
2. In a separate bowl, whisk the egg and milk together until well combined.
3. Gradually add the wet ingredients to the dry ingredients, stirring until you have a smooth batter. Be careful not to overmix, as this can lead to tough pancakes.
4. Heat a non-stick frying pan or griddle over medium heat. Add a small amount of butter or oil to grease the pan.
5. Once the pan is hot, spoon small dollops of batter onto the surface to form pancakes, about 2-3 inches (5-7cm) in diameter. You can make them larger if you prefer, but traditional Scotch pancakes are on the smaller side.
6. Cook the pancakes for 1-2 minutes on one side, or until bubbles start to form on the surface and the edges look set.
7. Flip the pancakes over using a spatula and cook for another 1-2 minutes on the other side, or until golden brown and cooked through.
8. Transfer the cooked pancakes to a plate and keep warm while you cook the remaining batter. You may need to adjust the heat of the pan as you go to prevent the pancakes from burning.
9. Serve the Scotch pancakes warm, stacked high and topped with butter, syrup, jam, or your favorite toppings.

Scotch pancakes are delicious served for breakfast or brunch, and they're sure to be a hit with the whole family. Enjoy your homemade Scotch pancakes!

Kedgeree

Ingredients:

- 1 cup (200g) long-grain white rice
- 2 cups (480ml) water
- 1 lb (450g) smoked haddock or other flaky white fish
- 4 eggs
- 2 tablespoons unsalted butter
- 1 onion, finely chopped
- 2 cloves garlic, minced
- 1 tablespoon curry powder
- 1 teaspoon ground cumin
- 1 teaspoon ground coriander
- 1/2 teaspoon turmeric
- 1/2 cup (120ml) chicken or vegetable broth
- Salt and pepper, to taste
- Fresh parsley or cilantro, chopped, for garnish
- Lemon wedges, for serving

Instructions:

1. Cook the rice: In a medium saucepan, combine the rice and water. Bring to a boil over medium-high heat, then reduce the heat to low, cover, and simmer for 15-20 minutes, or until the rice is tender and the water is absorbed. Remove from heat and let it sit, covered, for 5 minutes. Fluff the rice with a fork and set aside.
2. Prepare the fish and eggs: In a large skillet, place the smoked haddock (or other fish) and cover with water. Bring to a gentle simmer over medium heat and cook for about 5-7 minutes, or until the fish is cooked through and flakes easily with a fork. Remove the fish from the skillet and let it cool slightly before flaking it into bite-sized pieces, discarding any skin and bones. Hard-boil the eggs by placing them in a saucepan and covering with cold water. Bring to a boil over high heat, then reduce the heat to medium-low and simmer for 8-10 minutes. Drain the eggs, run them under cold water to cool, then peel and chop them.
3. Make the kedgeree: In the same skillet used to cook the fish, melt the butter over medium heat. Add the chopped onion and cook, stirring occasionally, until softened, about 5 minutes. Add the minced garlic, curry powder, ground cumin, ground coriander, and turmeric to the skillet. Cook, stirring constantly, for 1-2 minutes, or until fragrant.

4. Add the cooked rice, flaked fish, chopped eggs, and chicken or vegetable broth to the skillet. Stir gently to combine and heat through. Season with salt and pepper to taste.
5. Serve: Transfer the kedgeree to a serving dish and garnish with chopped fresh parsley or cilantro. Serve hot, with lemon wedges on the side for squeezing over the top.

Kedgeree makes a delicious and satisfying meal for breakfast, brunch, or dinner. Enjoy your homemade kedgeree!

Tablet

Ingredients:

- 2 cups (400g) granulated sugar
- 1 cup (225g) unsalted butter
- 1 can (14 oz/397g) sweetened condensed milk
- 1 teaspoon vanilla extract (optional)
- Pinch of salt

Instructions:

1. Prepare the pan: Line a 9x9 inch (23x23cm) baking pan with parchment paper, leaving some overhang on the sides for easy removal later. Grease the parchment paper with butter or cooking spray.
2. Cook the mixture: In a large, heavy-bottomed saucepan, combine the sugar, butter, condensed milk, and salt. Place the saucepan over medium heat and stir constantly until the butter has melted and the sugar has dissolved.
3. Boil the mixture: Once the mixture is smooth, increase the heat to medium-high and bring it to a rapid boil, stirring constantly. It's important to keep stirring to prevent the mixture from burning or sticking to the bottom of the pan.
4. Cook to the soft ball stage: Continue boiling the mixture, stirring constantly, until it reaches the soft ball stage, which is about 235-240°F (113-116°C) on a candy thermometer. If you don't have a candy thermometer, you can test for the soft ball stage by dropping a small amount of the mixture into a bowl of cold water. It should form a soft, pliable ball that holds its shape but flattens easily when pressed between your fingers.
5. Flavor the tablet (optional): Remove the saucepan from the heat and stir in the vanilla extract or any other flavorings you're using. Be careful, as the mixture will be very hot.
6. Beat the mixture: Using a wooden spoon or silicone spatula, beat the mixture vigorously for 5-10 minutes, or until it starts to thicken and lose its glossiness. This step is what gives tablet its crumbly texture.
7. Pour and cool: Quickly pour the mixture into the prepared baking pan and smooth it out into an even layer with a spatula.
8. Score and cool: While the tablet is still warm, use a sharp knife to score it into squares or rectangles. This will make it easier to cut later. Let the tablet cool completely in the pan at room temperature.

9. Cut and serve: Once the tablet is completely cooled and set, use the parchment paper overhang to lift it out of the pan. Cut it into pieces along the scored lines. Enjoy your homemade tablet as a sweet treat or gift it to friends and family!

Tablet is a deliciously sweet and indulgent treat that's perfect for special occasions or as a homemade gift. Enjoy making and sharing it with loved ones!

Clootie Dumpling

Ingredients:

- 2 cups (250g) all-purpose flour
- 1 cup (120g) breadcrumbs
- 1 cup (150g) mixed dried fruit (such as raisins, currants, and sultanas)
- 1/2 cup (75g) shredded suet (vegetarian suet can be used for a meat-free version)
- 1/2 cup (100g) brown sugar
- 1 teaspoon ground cinnamon
- 1/2 teaspoon ground ginger
- 1/4 teaspoon ground nutmeg
- 1/4 teaspoon ground cloves
- 1/4 teaspoon salt
- 1/2 cup (120ml) milk
- 1 large egg, beaten
- Butter or margarine, for greasing
- Additional flour, for dusting

Instructions:

1. Prepare the cloot: Begin by preparing a clean, cotton cloth (or "cloot") for boiling the dumpling. Rinse the cloth under cold water, then wring it out and dust it liberally with flour. Shake off any excess flour.
2. Mix the dry ingredients: In a large mixing bowl, combine the flour, breadcrumbs, mixed dried fruit, shredded suet, brown sugar, ground cinnamon, ground ginger, ground nutmeg, ground cloves, and salt. Mix well to combine.
3. Add the wet ingredients: In a separate bowl, whisk together the milk and beaten egg. Gradually add the wet ingredients to the dry ingredients, stirring until a thick, sticky dough forms. You may not need to use all of the milk mixture, so add it gradually until the dough comes together.
4. Boil the dumpling: Bring a large pot of water to a boil over high heat. Meanwhile, shape the dough into a round dumpling, about the size of a small melon. Place the dumpling in the center of the prepared cloth, then gather up the edges of the cloth and tie them securely with kitchen twine, leaving a little room for the dumpling to expand during cooking.

5. Carefully lower the dumpling into the boiling water, making sure it is fully submerged. Reduce the heat to medium-low and simmer the dumpling gently, covered, for 2-3 hours, or until it is cooked through and firm to the touch. Check the water level occasionally and top up with boiling water if necessary to keep the dumpling submerged.
6. Serve the dumpling: Once the dumpling is cooked, carefully remove it from the water and let it cool slightly before unwrapping it from the cloth. Slice the dumpling into thick slices and serve warm with custard, cream, or your favorite dessert sauce.

Clootie dumpling is a deliciously comforting dessert that's perfect for special occasions or as a festive treat. Enjoy making and sharing it with friends and family!

Partan Bree

Ingredients:

- 2 tablespoons butter or vegetable oil
- 1 onion, finely chopped
- 2 stalks celery, finely chopped
- 2 carrots, finely chopped
- 2 cloves garlic, minced
- 2 tablespoons all-purpose flour
- 4 cups (1 liter) fish or seafood stock
- 1 lb (450g) crab meat (fresh, canned, or frozen)
- 1 cup (240ml) heavy cream or milk
- 1 tablespoon chopped fresh parsley
- Salt and pepper, to taste
- Optional: cooked rice or barley, for serving
- Lemon wedges, for serving

Instructions:

1. Prepare the vegetables: In a large soup pot or Dutch oven, heat the butter or oil over medium heat. Add the chopped onion, celery, and carrots to the pot and cook, stirring occasionally, until the vegetables are softened, about 5-7 minutes. Add the minced garlic and cook for an additional 1-2 minutes, or until fragrant.
2. Make the broth: Sprinkle the flour over the cooked vegetables and stir well to combine. Cook for 1-2 minutes to cook off the raw flour taste. Gradually pour in the fish or seafood stock, stirring constantly to prevent lumps from forming. Bring the mixture to a simmer and cook for 5-10 minutes, or until slightly thickened.
3. Add the crab meat: Stir in the crab meat and continue to simmer for an additional 5 minutes, or until the crab is heated through.
4. Finish the soup: Stir in the heavy cream or milk and chopped parsley. Season the soup with salt and pepper to taste. If desired, add cooked rice or barley to the soup for extra heartiness.
5. Serve: Ladle the partan bree into bowls and garnish with additional chopped parsley, if desired. Serve hot, with lemon wedges on the side for squeezing over the soup.

Partan bree is a delicious and comforting soup that's perfect for a cozy meal on a cold day. Enjoy your homemade partan bree with crusty bread or crackers for dipping!

Finnan Haddie

Ingredients:

- 1 lb (450g) Finnan Haddie (cold-smoked haddock)
- Water, for soaking
- Milk, for poaching (optional)
- Butter, for serving (optional)
- Lemon wedges, for serving (optional)
- Fresh parsley, chopped, for garnish (optional)

Instructions:

1. Soak the Finnan Haddie: Place the Finnan Haddie in a bowl or shallow dish and cover it with cold water. Let it soak for at least 1 hour, or overnight in the refrigerator, to remove some of the saltiness and smokiness.
2. Poach the Finnan Haddie: After soaking, drain the Finnan Haddie and rinse it under cold water. If desired, you can poach the haddock in milk to add extra flavor and richness. Place the Finnan Haddie in a saucepan and cover it with milk. Bring the milk to a gentle simmer over medium heat and poach the haddock for about 10-15 minutes, or until it is cooked through and flakes easily with a fork.
3. Serve: Once the Finnan Haddie is cooked, remove it from the poaching liquid and transfer it to a serving plate. You can serve it simply with butter, lemon wedges, and chopped fresh parsley for garnish. Alternatively, you can incorporate it into other dishes like kedgeree or use it in omelettes or salads.
4. Enjoy: Finnan Haddie is best enjoyed hot or warm. Serve it immediately as part of a breakfast or brunch spread, or incorporate it into your favorite recipes for added flavor and texture.

Finnan Haddie is a delicious and versatile ingredient that adds a smoky twist to a variety of dishes. Enjoy exploring different ways to enjoy this traditional Scottish delicacy!

Smoked Salmon with Whisky Sauce

Ingredients:

- 4 slices smoked salmon
- 2 tablespoons butter
- 1 shallot, finely chopped
- 1/4 cup (60ml) whisky
- 1/2 cup (120ml) heavy cream
- 1 tablespoon Dijon mustard
- 1 tablespoon honey
- Salt and pepper, to taste
- Fresh dill or chives, chopped, for garnish (optional)
- Lemon wedges, for serving

Instructions:

1. Prepare the smoked salmon: Arrange the smoked salmon slices on serving plates or a platter. You can fold the slices into rolls or leave them flat, depending on your preference.
2. Make the whisky sauce: In a small saucepan, melt the butter over medium heat. Add the finely chopped shallot to the pan and cook, stirring occasionally, until softened, about 3-5 minutes.
3. Carefully add the whisky to the saucepan, stirring to deglaze the pan and incorporate any browned bits from the bottom. Let the whisky simmer for a minute or two to cook off some of the alcohol.
4. Stir in the heavy cream, Dijon mustard, and honey. Reduce the heat to low and simmer the sauce gently for 5-7 minutes, or until it thickens slightly. Season with salt and pepper to taste.
5. Serve: Spoon the warm whisky sauce over the smoked salmon slices. Garnish with chopped fresh dill or chives, if desired. Serve immediately, with lemon wedges on the side for squeezing over the salmon.
6. Enjoy: Smoked salmon with whisky sauce makes a delicious appetizer or light meal. Serve it with crusty bread or crackers for dipping, or alongside a fresh salad for a more substantial dish.

This dish is perfect for special occasions or as an elegant appetizer for entertaining guests. The combination of smoky salmon and creamy whisky sauce is sure to impress!

Bannock

Ingredients:

- 2 cups (250g) all-purpose flour
- 1 tablespoon baking powder
- 1/2 teaspoon salt
- 2 tablespoons butter or vegetable oil
- 3/4 cup (180ml) milk or water

Instructions:

1. In a large mixing bowl, whisk together the flour, baking powder, and salt.
2. Cut in the butter or vegetable oil using a pastry cutter or your fingers until the mixture resembles coarse crumbs.
3. Gradually add the milk or water to the dry ingredients, stirring until a soft dough forms. You may need to adjust the amount of liquid slightly depending on the humidity and other factors.
4. Turn the dough out onto a lightly floured surface and knead it gently for a minute or two until smooth. Avoid over-kneading, as this can make the bannock tough.
5. Divide the dough into equal portions and shape each portion into a round flatbread, about 1/2 inch (1.25cm) thick.
6. Heat a skillet or griddle over medium heat. Add a little oil or butter to the skillet.
7. Cook the bannock rounds for 2-3 minutes on each side, or until golden brown and cooked through. You may need to adjust the heat to prevent burning.
8. Serve the bannock warm, either plain or with butter, jam, honey, or other toppings of your choice.

Bannock is a versatile bread that can be enjoyed as a side dish with soups, stews, or chili, or eaten on its own as a snack or breakfast bread. It's a delicious and easy-to-make bread that's perfect for sharing with family and friends!

Stornoway Black Pudding

Ingredients:

- Stornoway Black Pudding (available from specialty food stores or online)
- Butter or oil, for frying (optional)

Instructions:

1. Prepare the black pudding: Stornoway Black Pudding is usually sold in a sausage-like shape. Depending on your preference, you can slice it into rounds or remove the casing and crumble it.
2. Cook the black pudding: Heat a skillet or frying pan over medium heat. If using, add a small amount of butter or oil to the pan. Once hot, add the black pudding slices or crumbles to the pan.
3. Fry the black pudding for 3-5 minutes on each side, or until heated through and nicely browned. Be careful not to overcook it, as black pudding can become dry if cooked for too long.
4. Serve: Once the black pudding is cooked to your liking, remove it from the pan and transfer it to a serving plate. It's often served alongside other breakfast items such as bacon, eggs, sausages, tomatoes, and mushrooms.
5. Enjoy: Stornoway Black Pudding is best enjoyed hot and fresh. Serve it as part of a hearty Scottish breakfast or use it as an ingredient in other dishes such as salads, pies, or even pasta.

Stornoway Black Pudding is loved for its unique flavor and texture, which comes from a combination of spices, oatmeal, and, of course, blood. It's a delicious and versatile ingredient that adds depth and richness to any meal.

Leek and Potato Soup

Ingredients:

- 2 tablespoons butter or olive oil
- 3 leeks, white and light green parts only, thinly sliced
- 3 medium potatoes, peeled and diced
- 4 cups (1 liter) vegetable or chicken broth
- 1 bay leaf
- Salt and pepper, to taste
- 1/2 cup (120ml) heavy cream or milk (optional)
- Fresh chives or parsley, chopped, for garnish (optional)

Instructions:

1. Prepare the leeks: Trim off the roots and dark green tops of the leeks. Slice them in half lengthwise and rinse them under cold water to remove any dirt or grit trapped between the layers. Pat them dry with a clean kitchen towel and thinly slice them.
2. Cook the leeks: In a large pot or Dutch oven, heat the butter or olive oil over medium heat. Add the sliced leeks to the pot and cook, stirring occasionally, until softened, about 5-7 minutes.
3. Add the potatoes: Add the diced potatoes to the pot with the leeks and cook for an additional 2-3 minutes, stirring occasionally.
4. Simmer the soup: Pour the vegetable or chicken broth into the pot, along with the bay leaf. Bring the soup to a boil, then reduce the heat to low and simmer, covered, for about 15-20 minutes, or until the potatoes are tender.
5. Blend the soup: Once the potatoes are cooked through, remove the bay leaf from the pot. Use an immersion blender to puree the soup until smooth and creamy. Alternatively, you can carefully transfer the soup in batches to a blender and blend until smooth, then return it to the pot.
6. Adjust the consistency: If the soup is too thick, you can thin it out with a little more broth or water. If desired, stir in the heavy cream or milk to add richness to the soup. Season with salt and pepper to taste.
7. Serve: Ladle the soup into bowls and garnish with chopped fresh chives or parsley, if using. Serve hot, with crusty bread or crackers on the side.

Leek and potato soup is a delicious and satisfying dish that's perfect for lunch or dinner. It's also a great way to incorporate more vegetables into your diet. Enjoy your homemade soup!

Highland Beef Stew

Ingredients:

- 2 lbs (900g) beef stew meat, cut into bite-sized pieces
- 2 tablespoons all-purpose flour
- Salt and pepper, to taste
- 2 tablespoons vegetable oil
- 1 onion, chopped
- 2 cloves garlic, minced
- 4 carrots, peeled and chopped
- 2 parsnips, peeled and chopped
- 2 potatoes, peeled and chopped
- 1 cup (240ml) beef broth
- 1 cup (240ml) stout beer (such as Guinness)
- 2 tablespoons tomato paste
- 1 tablespoon Worcestershire sauce
- 1 teaspoon dried thyme
- 1 teaspoon dried rosemary
- 1 bay leaf
- Chopped fresh parsley, for garnish (optional)

Instructions:

1. Preheat the oven: Preheat your oven to 325°F (160°C).
2. Coat the beef: In a large bowl, toss the beef stew meat with the flour, salt, and pepper until evenly coated.
3. Brown the beef: Heat the vegetable oil in a large Dutch oven or oven-safe pot over medium-high heat. Add the beef to the pot in batches and cook until browned on all sides, about 5-7 minutes per batch. Transfer the browned beef to a plate and set aside.
4. Sauté the vegetables: Add the chopped onion to the pot and cook, stirring occasionally, until softened, about 5 minutes. Add the minced garlic and cook for an additional 1-2 minutes. Add the chopped carrots, parsnips, and potatoes to the pot and cook for another 5 minutes, stirring occasionally.
5. Deglaze the pot: Pour the beef broth and stout beer into the pot, using a wooden spoon to scrape up any browned bits from the bottom of the pot. Stir in the tomato paste, Worcestershire sauce, dried thyme, dried rosemary, and bay leaf.

6. Add the beef: Return the browned beef to the pot and stir to combine everything evenly.
7. Bake the stew: Cover the pot with a lid and transfer it to the preheated oven. Bake for 2-3 hours, or until the beef is tender and the vegetables are cooked through.
8. Serve: Once the stew is ready, remove the bay leaf and discard it. Ladle the stew into bowls and garnish with chopped fresh parsley, if desired. Serve hot, with crusty bread or biscuits on the side.

Highland beef stew is a comforting and hearty dish that's perfect for warming you up on a cold day. Enjoy making and sharing it with friends and family!

Cranberry and Orange Scones

Ingredients:

- 2 cups (250g) all-purpose flour
- 1/4 cup (50g) granulated sugar
- 1 tablespoon baking powder
- 1/2 teaspoon salt
- Zest of 1 orange
- 1/2 cup (115g) unsalted butter, cold and cubed
- 1/2 cup (120ml) heavy cream, plus extra for brushing
- 1 large egg
- 1 teaspoon vanilla extract
- 1/2 cup (60g) dried cranberries
- Optional: coarse sugar, for sprinkling

Instructions:

1. Preheat the oven: Preheat your oven to 400°F (200°C). Line a baking sheet with parchment paper or silicone baking mat.
2. Prepare the dry ingredients: In a large mixing bowl, whisk together the flour, sugar, baking powder, salt, and orange zest until well combined.
3. Cut in the butter: Add the cold, cubed butter to the dry ingredients. Use a pastry cutter or your fingers to cut the butter into the flour mixture until it resembles coarse crumbs with some pea-sized pieces of butter remaining.
4. Mix the wet ingredients: In a separate small bowl, whisk together the heavy cream, egg, and vanilla extract until well combined.
5. Combine the dough: Pour the wet ingredients into the dry ingredients, along with the dried cranberries. Stir gently with a fork or spatula until the dough starts to come together.
6. Knead the dough: Turn the dough out onto a lightly floured surface. Gently knead it a few times until it comes together, being careful not to overwork the dough.
7. Shape the scones: Pat the dough into a circle about 1 inch (2.5cm) thick. Use a sharp knife or a bench scraper to cut the dough into 8 equal wedges.
8. Bake the scones: Transfer the scones to the prepared baking sheet, leaving some space between each one. Brush the tops of the scones with a little heavy cream and sprinkle with coarse sugar, if desired.
9. **Bake in the preheated oven for 15-18 minutes, or until the scones are golden brown and cooked through.

10. Serve: Allow the scones to cool slightly on the baking sheet before transferring them to a wire rack to cool completely. Enjoy warm or at room temperature, with clotted cream, jam, or butter.

These cranberry and orange scones are best enjoyed fresh on the day they are made, but they can also be stored in an airtight container at room temperature for up to 2 days. Simply reheat them in the oven or microwave before serving, if desired. Enjoy!

Skirlie

Ingredients:

- 1 cup (90g) steel-cut oats or pinhead oats
- 2 tablespoons butter or vegetable oil
- 1 large onion, finely chopped
- Salt and pepper, to taste
- Optional: chopped fresh herbs such as parsley or thyme

Instructions:

1. Toast the oats: Place the steel-cut oats in a dry skillet or frying pan over medium heat. Toast the oats, stirring constantly, for about 5-7 minutes, or until they are lightly golden and fragrant. Be careful not to let them burn. Remove the toasted oats from the skillet and set them aside.
2. Cook the onions: In the same skillet, melt the butter or heat the vegetable oil over medium heat. Add the chopped onion to the skillet and cook, stirring occasionally, until the onions are soft and translucent, about 5-7 minutes.
3. Add the oats: Return the toasted oats to the skillet with the cooked onions. Stir well to combine and coat the oats with the onions and butter or oil.
4. Season the skirlie: Season the skirlie with salt and pepper to taste. You can also add chopped fresh herbs like parsley or thyme for extra flavor if desired.
5. Cook until golden: Continue to cook the skirlie, stirring occasionally, for an additional 5-10 minutes, or until the oats are cooked through and golden brown. The skirlie should have a slightly crispy texture on the outside while remaining tender on the inside.
6. Serve: Once the skirlie is cooked to your liking, remove it from the skillet and transfer it to a serving dish. Serve hot as a side dish or stuffing alongside your favorite meat dishes, such as haggis or roasted meats.

Skirlie is a delicious and versatile dish that adds a hearty and flavorful element to any meal. Enjoy experimenting with different variations and serving it alongside your favorite Scottish dishes!

Scottish Oatcakes

Ingredients:

- 1 cup (90g) oatmeal (rolled oats or pinhead oats)
- 1/2 cup (60g) all-purpose flour
- 1/2 teaspoon baking soda
- 1/2 teaspoon salt
- 2 tablespoons cold butter, diced
- 2-3 tablespoons boiling water

Instructions:

1. Preheat the oven: Preheat your oven to 350°F (180°C). Line a baking sheet with parchment paper or lightly grease it.
2. Prepare the dry ingredients: In a large mixing bowl, combine the oatmeal, all-purpose flour, baking soda, and salt. Mix well to ensure the ingredients are evenly distributed.
3. Cut in the butter: Add the diced cold butter to the dry ingredients. Use your fingertips or a pastry cutter to rub or cut the butter into the flour mixture until it resembles coarse crumbs.
4. Add the water: Gradually add the boiling water to the mixture, stirring with a spoon or your hands until a soft dough forms. You may need to adjust the amount of water slightly depending on the consistency of your dough.
5. Roll out the dough: Transfer the dough to a lightly floured surface. Roll it out to a thickness of about 1/4 inch (6mm).
6. Cut into rounds: Use a cookie cutter or the rim of a glass to cut the dough into rounds. Alternatively, you can shape the dough into rounds by hand and flatten them slightly.
7. Bake the oatcakes: Place the rounds on the prepared baking sheet. Bake in the preheated oven for 15-20 minutes, or until the oatcakes are lightly golden and firm to the touch.
8. Cool and store: Remove the oatcakes from the oven and transfer them to a wire rack to cool completely. Once cooled, store the oatcakes in an airtight container at room temperature for up to one week.

Scottish oatcakes are delicious served on their own or topped with butter, cheese, jam, or any other toppings of your choice. They're a versatile and wholesome snack that's perfect for any time of day. Enjoy!

Rumbledethumps

Ingredients:

- 2 lbs (about 900g) potatoes, peeled and diced
- 1 small head of cabbage, cored and thinly sliced
- 1 large onion, finely chopped
- 2 tablespoons butter
- 1 cup (about 120g) grated cheese (such as cheddar or Scottish cheese)
- Salt and pepper, to taste
- Optional: breadcrumbs, for topping

Instructions:

1. Prepare the potatoes: Place the diced potatoes in a large pot and cover them with water. Bring the water to a boil, then reduce the heat to medium-low and simmer the potatoes until they are tender, about 15-20 minutes.
2. Cook the cabbage and onions: While the potatoes are cooking, heat the butter in a large skillet over medium heat. Add the chopped onion to the skillet and cook, stirring occasionally, until softened and translucent, about 5-7 minutes. Add the sliced cabbage to the skillet and continue to cook, stirring occasionally, until the cabbage is wilted and tender, about 8-10 minutes.
3. Mash the potatoes: Once the potatoes are cooked, drain them well and return them to the pot. Use a potato masher or fork to mash the potatoes until smooth and creamy.
4. Combine the ingredients: Add the cooked cabbage and onions to the mashed potatoes, along with the grated cheese. Stir well to combine all the ingredients. Season the mixture with salt and pepper to taste.
5. Assemble the rumbledethumps: Transfer the potato and cabbage mixture to a greased baking dish, spreading it out evenly. If desired, sprinkle breadcrumbs over the top of the mixture for added texture.
6. Bake the rumbledethumps: Place the baking dish in a preheated oven and bake at 375°F (190°C) for 25-30 minutes, or until the top is golden brown and the mixture is heated through.
7. Serve: Once baked, remove the rumbledethumps from the oven and let them cool slightly before serving. Serve hot as a side dish or main course, accompanied by additional vegetables, gravy, or your favorite condiments.

Rumbledethumps is a delicious and satisfying dish that's perfect for a cozy meal on a cold day. Enjoy making and sharing it with family and friends!

Stuffed Sheep's Stomach (a variation of haggis)

Ingredients:

- 1 sheep's stomach (available from specialty butchers or online)
- 1 sheep's liver, minced
- 1 sheep's heart, minced
- 1 sheep's lung (if available), minced
- 1 large onion, finely chopped
- 1 cup (120g) steel-cut oats or pinhead oats
- 1/2 cup (115g) beef suet, finely chopped or grated
- 1 teaspoon salt
- 1/2 teaspoon black pepper
- 1/2 teaspoon ground coriander
- 1/4 teaspoon ground nutmeg
- 1/4 teaspoon ground cloves
- 1/4 teaspoon ground allspice
- 1/4 teaspoon ground ginger
- 1/4 teaspoon ground mace
- 1/4 teaspoon ground cinnamon
- 1/4 cup (60ml) beef or vegetable broth (optional, for moistening)

Instructions:

1. Prepare the sheep's stomach: Rinse the sheep's stomach thoroughly under cold water. Turn it inside out and scrape away any excess fat or residue. Place the stomach in a large pot of cold water and bring it to a boil. Boil the stomach for 1-2 hours, then remove it from the water and set it aside to cool.
2. Prepare the filling: In a large mixing bowl, combine the minced liver, heart, lung (if using), and finely chopped onion. Add the steel-cut oats, beef suet, salt, pepper, and spices to the bowl. Mix everything together until well combined. If the mixture seems too dry, you can add a little beef or vegetable broth to moisten it.
3. Stuff the stomach: Once the sheep's stomach has cooled slightly, spoon the filling mixture into it, filling it about three-quarters full. Be careful not to overfill the stomach, as the filling will expand during cooking.
4. Sew or tie the stomach: Using kitchen twine or a needle and thread, sew the opening of the sheep's stomach closed to secure the filling inside. Alternatively, you can tie the opening with kitchen twine to seal it shut.

5. Boil the stuffed stomach: Place the stuffed sheep's stomach in a large pot and cover it with water. Bring the water to a boil, then reduce the heat to low and simmer the stomach for 3-4 hours, or until the filling is cooked through and the stomach is tender.
6. Serve: Once cooked, remove the stuffed sheep's stomach from the pot and let it cool slightly before slicing it into portions. Serve hot with mashed potatoes, neeps and tatties, or your favorite accompaniments.

Stuffed sheep's stomach is a traditional and hearty dish that's perfect for celebrating Scottish cuisine and culture. While it may require some special ingredients and preparation techniques, it's sure to be a memorable and delicious addition to any meal. Enjoy making and sharing it with family and friends!

Scones with Clotted Cream and Jam

Ingredients for Scones:

- 2 cups (250g) all-purpose flour
- 1/4 cup (50g) granulated sugar
- 1 tablespoon baking powder
- 1/2 teaspoon salt
- 1/3 cup (75g) cold unsalted butter, cut into small pieces
- 1/2 cup (120ml) milk
- 1 large egg
- 1 teaspoon vanilla extract

For Serving:

- Clotted cream
- Jam (traditionally strawberry or raspberry)
- Additional butter (optional)

Instructions:

1. Preheat the oven: Preheat your oven to 400°F (200°C). Line a baking sheet with parchment paper or lightly grease it.
2. Prepare the dry ingredients: In a large mixing bowl, whisk together the flour, sugar, baking powder, and salt until well combined.
3. Cut in the butter: Add the cold butter pieces to the dry ingredients. Use a pastry cutter or your fingertips to rub the butter into the flour mixture until it resembles coarse crumbs.
4. Mix the wet ingredients: In a separate small bowl, whisk together the milk, egg, and vanilla extract until well combined.
5. Combine the dough: Pour the wet ingredients into the dry ingredients. Stir gently with a spoon or spatula until the mixture comes together to form a soft dough. Be careful not to overmix.
6. Shape the scones: Turn the dough out onto a lightly floured surface. Pat it into a circle about 1 inch (2.5cm) thick. Use a round cutter (about 2-3 inches in diameter) to cut out the scones. Place the scones on the prepared baking sheet, leaving some space between each one.

7. Bake the scones: Brush the tops of the scones with a little milk or beaten egg for a golden finish (optional). Bake in the preheated oven for 12-15 minutes, or until the scones are risen and golden brown.
8. Serve: Once baked, remove the scones from the oven and transfer them to a wire rack to cool slightly. Serve warm with clotted cream, jam, and additional butter if desired.

To enjoy scones with clotted cream and jam, split the warm scones in half and spread each half with a generous dollop of clotted cream followed by a spoonful of jam. Serve alongside a pot of tea for a delightful and indulgent treat!

Feel free to customize the scones by adding dried fruit, citrus zest, or other flavorings to the dough if desired. Enjoy!

Scottish Salmon Pie

Ingredients:

For the filling:

- 1 lb (450g) salmon fillets, skin removed, cut into bite-sized pieces
- 1 tablespoon olive oil
- 1 onion, finely chopped
- 2 cloves garlic, minced
- 1 cup (240ml) fish or vegetable broth
- 1 cup (240ml) heavy cream
- 2 tablespoons all-purpose flour
- 1 tablespoon Dijon mustard
- 1 tablespoon fresh dill, chopped
- Salt and pepper, to taste
- Juice of 1/2 lemon

For the pastry:

- 1 sheet of store-bought puff pastry, thawed if frozen
- 1 egg, beaten (for egg wash)

Instructions:

1. Prepare the filling: In a large skillet, heat the olive oil over medium heat. Add the chopped onion and garlic to the skillet and cook, stirring occasionally, until softened, about 5 minutes.
2. Add the salmon pieces to the skillet and cook for 2-3 minutes, stirring gently, until lightly browned on all sides.
3. In a small bowl, whisk together the fish or vegetable broth, heavy cream, flour, Dijon mustard, chopped dill, salt, pepper, and lemon juice until smooth.
4. Pour the cream mixture into the skillet with the salmon and onions. Bring the mixture to a simmer and cook for 5-7 minutes, stirring occasionally, until the sauce has thickened slightly and the salmon is cooked through. Remove the skillet from the heat and let the filling cool slightly.

5. Prepare the pastry: Preheat your oven to 400°F (200°C). Roll out the puff pastry sheet on a lightly floured surface to fit the size of your pie dish. Place the rolled-out pastry into the pie dish, trimming any excess pastry from the edges.
6. Assemble the pie: Pour the cooled salmon filling into the pastry-lined pie dish, spreading it out evenly. Brush the edges of the pastry with beaten egg to create a seal.
7. Roll out the remaining pastry sheet and place it over the top of the pie. Press the edges of the pastry together to seal, then trim any excess pastry.
8. Brush the top of the pastry with beaten egg for a golden finish.
9. Bake the pie: Place the pie in the preheated oven and bake for 25-30 minutes, or until the pastry is golden brown and crispy.
10. Serve: Once baked, remove the pie from the oven and let it cool for a few minutes before slicing and serving. Enjoy your Scottish salmon pie warm, with a side of mashed potatoes and greens, if desired.

This Scottish salmon pie is sure to be a hit with its creamy filling and flaky pastry crust.

It's perfect for a cozy dinner or special occasion. Enjoy!

Scottish Salmon Fillets with Lemon and Dill

Ingredients:

- 4 salmon fillets (about 6 oz/170g each), skin-on or skinless
- Salt and pepper, to taste
- 2 tablespoons olive oil
- 2 cloves garlic, minced
- Zest of 1 lemon
- Juice of 1 lemon
- 2 tablespoons fresh dill, chopped
- Lemon wedges, for serving

Instructions:

1. Preheat the oven: Preheat your oven to 400°F (200°C). Line a baking sheet with parchment paper or aluminum foil.
2. Season the salmon: Pat the salmon fillets dry with paper towels. Season both sides of the fillets with salt and pepper, to taste.
3. Prepare the lemon and dill mixture: In a small bowl, whisk together the olive oil, minced garlic, lemon zest, lemon juice, and chopped fresh dill.
4. Marinate the salmon: Place the seasoned salmon fillets on the prepared baking sheet. Pour the lemon and dill mixture over the fillets, making sure they are evenly coated.
5. Bake the salmon: Transfer the baking sheet to the preheated oven and bake the salmon for 12-15 minutes, or until the fillets are cooked through and flake easily with a fork. Cooking time may vary depending on the thickness of the fillets.
6. Serve: Once baked, remove the salmon fillets from the oven and let them rest for a few minutes. Serve the salmon hot, garnished with additional fresh dill and lemon wedges on the side.
7. Optional: For an extra burst of flavor, you can sprinkle some additional lemon zest over the cooked salmon just before serving.

This dish pairs well with a variety of side dishes, such as steamed vegetables, roasted potatoes, or a fresh salad. It's a quick and easy recipe that's perfect for a weeknight dinner or special occasion. Enjoy your Scottish salmon fillets with lemon and dill!

Vegetarian Haggis

Ingredients:

- 1 cup (200g) dried red lentils, rinsed
- 2 cups (480ml) vegetable broth or water
- 2 tablespoons olive oil
- 1 onion, finely chopped
- 2 cloves garlic, minced
- 1 carrot, grated
- 1 celery stalk, finely chopped
- 1/2 cup (75g) mushrooms, finely chopped
- 1/2 cup (75g) cooked kidney beans, mashed
- 1/2 cup (50g) rolled oats
- 1/4 cup (30g) toasted walnuts or hazelnuts, chopped
- 2 tablespoons soy sauce or tamari
- 1 tablespoon tomato paste
- 1 teaspoon dried thyme
- 1 teaspoon dried rosemary
- 1/2 teaspoon ground black pepper
- 1/4 teaspoon ground nutmeg
- Salt, to taste
- 1/4 cup (60ml) whiskey (optional)

Instructions:

1. Cook the lentils: In a medium saucepan, combine the rinsed red lentils and vegetable broth or water. Bring to a boil, then reduce the heat to low and simmer for 20-25 minutes, or until the lentils are soft and cooked through. Drain any excess liquid and set aside.
2. Prepare the filling: In a large skillet, heat the olive oil over medium heat. Add the chopped onion and garlic to the skillet and cook, stirring occasionally, until softened and translucent, about 5 minutes.
3. Add the grated carrot, chopped celery, and chopped mushrooms to the skillet. Cook, stirring occasionally, for another 5-7 minutes, or until the vegetables are tender.
4. Combine the ingredients: In a large mixing bowl, combine the cooked lentils, sautéed vegetables, mashed kidney beans, rolled oats, chopped nuts, soy sauce,

tomato paste, dried thyme, dried rosemary, black pepper, nutmeg, and salt to taste. Mix well to combine all the ingredients evenly.
5. Optional: Add whiskey: If using whiskey, pour it over the mixture and stir until well combined. The whiskey adds depth of flavor to the haggis, but you can omit it if preferred.
6. Bake the haggis: Preheat your oven to 350°F (180°C). Transfer the haggis mixture to a greased baking dish and press it down evenly with a spatula or the back of a spoon.
7. **Cover the baking dish with aluminum foil and bake the haggis in the preheated oven for 30-40 minutes, or until heated through and golden brown on top.
8. Serve: Once baked, remove the vegetarian haggis from the oven and let it cool for a few minutes before slicing and serving. Enjoy your vegetarian haggis with neeps and tatties (mashed turnips and potatoes) and a drizzle of whiskey sauce, if desired.

This vegetarian haggis recipe is packed with hearty lentils, vegetables, and flavorful herbs and spices, making it a delicious and nutritious alternative to traditional haggis. Enjoy making and sharing it with family and friends!

Venison Pie

Ingredients:

For the filling:

- 2 lbs (about 900g) venison stew meat, diced
- 2 tablespoons olive oil
- 1 onion, diced
- 2 cloves garlic, minced
- 2 carrots, diced
- 2 celery stalks, diced
- 8 oz (225g) mushrooms, sliced
- 2 tablespoons all-purpose flour
- 2 cups (480ml) beef or venison broth
- 1/2 cup (120ml) red wine
- 2 tablespoons tomato paste
- 1 tablespoon Worcestershire sauce
- 1 teaspoon dried thyme
- 1 teaspoon dried rosemary
- Salt and pepper, to taste

For the pastry:

- 2 sheets of store-bought puff pastry, thawed if frozen
- 1 egg, beaten (for egg wash)

Instructions:

1. Preheat the oven: Preheat your oven to 375°F (190°C).
2. Prepare the filling: In a large skillet or Dutch oven, heat the olive oil over medium heat. Add the diced venison stew meat and cook until browned on all sides. Remove the meat from the skillet and set aside.
3. In the same skillet, add the diced onion, minced garlic, carrots, and celery. Cook, stirring occasionally, until the vegetables are softened, about 5-7 minutes.
4. Add the sliced mushrooms to the skillet and cook for an additional 5 minutes, or until they are golden brown and tender.
5. Sprinkle the flour over the vegetables and stir well to coat. Cook for 1-2 minutes, then gradually stir in the beef or venison broth and red wine.

6. Stir in the tomato paste, Worcestershire sauce, dried thyme, dried rosemary, salt, and pepper. Bring the mixture to a simmer, then reduce the heat to low.
7. Return the browned venison stew meat to the skillet and stir to combine. Simmer the filling for 20-30 minutes, stirring occasionally, until the venison is tender and the sauce has thickened.
8. Assemble the pie: Transfer the venison filling to a deep pie dish or baking dish. Roll out one sheet of puff pastry on a lightly floured surface to fit the top of the pie dish. Place the pastry over the filling and trim any excess pastry from the edges.
9. Brush the edges of the pastry with beaten egg to create a seal. Roll out the second sheet of puff pastry and place it over the top of the pie. Press the edges of the pastry together to seal, then trim any excess pastry.
10. Bake the pie: Brush the top of the pastry with beaten egg for a golden finish. Cut a few slits in the top of the pastry to allow steam to escape during baking.
11. Place the pie in the preheated oven and bake for 30-35 minutes, or until the pastry is golden brown and crispy.
12. Serve: Once baked, remove the venison pie from the oven and let it cool for a few minutes before serving. Slice and serve hot, accompanied by mashed potatoes, steamed vegetables, or your favorite side dishes.

This venison pie is sure to be a hit with its tender meat and rich, flavorful filling encased in flaky puff pastry. Enjoy making and sharing it with family and friends!

Scotch Lamb Hotpot

Ingredients:

- 2 lbs (about 900g) lamb shoulder or leg meat, trimmed and diced
- 2 tablespoons vegetable oil
- 2 onions, thinly sliced
- 2 carrots, sliced
- 2 celery stalks, sliced
- 2 cloves garlic, minced
- 2 tablespoons all-purpose flour
- 2 cups (480ml) beef or lamb broth
- 2 tablespoons Worcestershire sauce
- 2 bay leaves
- Salt and pepper, to taste
- 4 large potatoes, peeled and thinly sliced
- 2 tablespoons butter, melted

Instructions:

1. Preheat the oven: Preheat your oven to 350°F (180°C).
2. Prepare the lamb: Season the diced lamb with salt and pepper. Heat the vegetable oil in a large ovenproof pot or Dutch oven over medium-high heat. Add the seasoned lamb to the pot and cook until browned on all sides. Remove the lamb from the pot and set aside.
3. Cook the vegetables: In the same pot, add the sliced onions, carrots, and celery. Cook, stirring occasionally, until the vegetables are softened, about 5-7 minutes. Add the minced garlic and cook for an additional minute.
4. Make the gravy: Sprinkle the flour over the cooked vegetables and stir well to coat. Cook for 1-2 minutes, then gradually pour in the beef or lamb broth, stirring constantly to prevent lumps from forming. Add the Worcestershire sauce and bay leaves, then return the browned lamb to the pot. Bring the mixture to a simmer, then reduce the heat to low. Cover and cook for 1-2 hours, or until the lamb is tender and the sauce has thickened.
5. Assemble the hotpot: Arrange the thinly sliced potatoes on top of the lamb mixture in the pot, overlapping them slightly. Brush the melted butter over the potatoes.

6. Bake the hotpot: Cover the pot with a lid or aluminum foil and transfer it to the preheated oven. Bake for 1-1.5 hours, or until the potatoes are tender and golden brown.
7. Serve: Once baked, remove the hotpot from the oven and let it cool for a few minutes before serving. Spoon the hotpot onto plates, making sure to include some of the tender lamb, vegetables, and potatoes in each serving. Enjoy your Scotch lamb hotpot hot, with crusty bread or a side salad if desired.

This Scotch lamb hotpot is sure to warm you up with its rich flavors and hearty ingredients. It's a classic comfort food that's perfect for sharing with family and friends on a cozy evening. Enjoy making and savoring this delicious dish!

Scotch Whisky Trifle

Ingredients:

For the sponge cake:

- 1 store-bought sponge cake or homemade sponge cake, cut into cubes
- 1/2 cup (120ml) Scotch whisky

For the custard:

- 2 cups (480ml) whole milk
- 4 egg yolks
- 1/3 cup (65g) granulated sugar
- 2 tablespoons cornstarch
- 1 teaspoon vanilla extract

For the fruit layer:

- 2 cups (300g) mixed berries (such as strawberries, raspberries, and blueberries)
- 2 tablespoons granulated sugar
- 2 tablespoons Scotch whisky

For the whipped cream:

- 1 cup (240ml) heavy cream
- 2 tablespoons powdered sugar
- 1 teaspoon vanilla extract

For garnish:

- Fresh berries
- Mint leaves

Instructions:

1. Prepare the sponge cake: Cut the sponge cake into cubes and place them in the bottom of a trifle dish or individual serving glasses. Drizzle the Scotch whisky over the sponge cake cubes, allowing them to soak up the liquor. Set aside.
2. Make the custard: In a medium saucepan, heat the milk over medium heat until it just begins to simmer. In a separate bowl, whisk together the egg yolks, sugar, and cornstarch until smooth and pale yellow.
3. Gradually pour the hot milk into the egg yolk mixture, whisking constantly to combine. Return the mixture to the saucepan and cook over medium heat, stirring constantly, until the custard thickens and coats the back of a spoon, about 5-7 minutes. Stir in the vanilla extract. Remove from heat and let the custard cool slightly.
4. Prepare the fruit layer: In a bowl, toss the mixed berries with granulated sugar and Scotch whisky until well coated. Let the berries macerate for about 10-15 minutes to release their juices.
5. Assemble the trifle: Spoon the custard over the soaked sponge cake cubes in the trifle dish or serving glasses, spreading it out evenly. Arrange the macerated berries over the custard layer.
6. Make the whipped cream: In a chilled mixing bowl, whip the heavy cream, powdered sugar, and vanilla extract until stiff peaks form.
7. Top the trifle: Spoon the whipped cream over the fruit layer, covering it completely. Smooth the top with a spatula.
8. Garnish: Garnish the trifle with fresh berries and mint leaves for a decorative touch.
9. Chill: Cover the trifle with plastic wrap and refrigerate for at least 2-3 hours, or until chilled and set.
10. Serve: Once chilled, serve the Scotch whisky trifle chilled, scooping out portions into dessert bowls or glasses.

This Scotch whisky trifle is a luxurious and indulgent dessert that's perfect for special occasions or holiday celebrations. Enjoy the layers of flavors and textures, from the moist sponge cake soaked in whisky to the creamy custard and fresh berries!

Scottish Steak Pie

Ingredients:

For the filling:

- 2 lbs (about 900g) stewing beef, cut into bite-sized pieces
- Salt and pepper, to taste
- 2 tablespoons vegetable oil
- 2 onions, chopped
- 2 carrots, diced
- 2 celery stalks, diced
- 2 cloves garlic, minced
- 2 tablespoons all-purpose flour
- 2 cups (480ml) beef broth
- 1 tablespoon Worcestershire sauce
- 1 teaspoon dried thyme
- 1 teaspoon dried rosemary
- 1 bay leaf
- Optional: 1/2 cup (120ml) ale or stout

For the pastry:

- 2 sheets of store-bought puff pastry, thawed if frozen
- 1 egg, beaten (for egg wash)

Instructions:

1. Preheat the oven: Preheat your oven to 375°F (190°C).
2. Prepare the filling: Season the beef pieces with salt and pepper. Heat the vegetable oil in a large ovenproof pot or Dutch oven over medium-high heat. Add the seasoned beef to the pot and cook until browned on all sides. Remove the beef from the pot and set aside.
3. In the same pot, add the chopped onions, diced carrots, and diced celery. Cook, stirring occasionally, until the vegetables are softened, about 5-7 minutes. Add the minced garlic and cook for an additional minute.

4. Sprinkle the flour over the cooked vegetables and stir well to coat. Cook for 1-2 minutes, then gradually pour in the beef broth, stirring constantly to prevent lumps from forming. Add the Worcestershire sauce, dried thyme, dried rosemary, and bay leaf. Return the browned beef to the pot. If using ale or stout, pour it into the pot as well. Bring the mixture to a simmer, then reduce the heat to low. Cover and cook for 1.5-2 hours, or until the beef is tender and the sauce has thickened.
5. Prepare the pastry: While the filling is cooking, roll out one sheet of puff pastry on a lightly floured surface to fit the top of your pie dish. Set aside.
6. Assemble the pie: Once the filling is ready, remove the bay leaf from the pot. Transfer the filling to a deep pie dish. Place the rolled-out puff pastry over the filling, pressing the edges to seal. Trim any excess pastry.
7. Brush the top of the pastry with beaten egg for a golden finish. Cut a few slits in the top of the pastry to allow steam to escape during baking.
8. Bake the pie: Place the pie dish on a baking sheet (to catch any drips) and transfer it to the preheated oven. Bake for 30-35 minutes, or until the pastry is golden brown and crispy.
9. Serve: Once baked, remove the steak pie from the oven and let it cool for a few minutes before serving. Slice and serve hot, accompanied by mashed potatoes, peas, or your favorite side dishes.

This Scottish steak pie is sure to be a hit with its tender beef and rich, flavorful gravy encased in flaky puff pastry. Enjoy making and sharing it with family and friends!

Potato and Leek Soup

Ingredients:

- 2 tablespoons butter or olive oil
- 3 leeks, white and light green parts only, thinly sliced
- 3 cloves garlic, minced
- 4 large potatoes, peeled and diced
- 4 cups (1 liter) vegetable or chicken broth
- 1 bay leaf
- Salt and pepper, to taste
- 1 cup (240ml) heavy cream (optional)
- Fresh chives or parsley, chopped, for garnish (optional)

Instructions:

1. Prepare the leeks: Trim off the roots and dark green tops of the leeks. Slice the leeks in half lengthwise and rinse them under cold water to remove any dirt or grit. Pat them dry and thinly slice.
2. Cook the leeks: In a large pot or Dutch oven, melt the butter over medium heat. Add the sliced leeks and minced garlic to the pot. Cook, stirring occasionally, until the leeks are softened, about 5-7 minutes.
3. Add the potatoes: Add the diced potatoes to the pot, along with the vegetable or chicken broth and bay leaf. Season with salt and pepper, to taste. Bring the mixture to a boil, then reduce the heat to low and simmer, covered, until the potatoes are tender, about 15-20 minutes.
4. Blend the soup: Once the potatoes are cooked through, remove the bay leaf from the pot. Use an immersion blender to blend the soup until smooth and creamy. Alternatively, transfer the soup in batches to a blender and blend until smooth, then return it to the pot.
5. Adjust the consistency: If the soup is too thick, you can add more broth or water to reach your desired consistency. If you prefer a creamier soup, stir in the heavy cream at this point.
6. Taste and adjust seasoning: Taste the soup and adjust the seasoning with salt and pepper, if needed.
7. Serve: Ladle the potato and leek soup into bowls. Garnish with chopped fresh chives or parsley, if desired. Serve hot, with crusty bread or croutons on the side, if desired.

This potato and leek soup is creamy, flavorful, and comforting—a perfect meal on its own or served as a starter. Enjoy making and savoring this delicious soup!

Smoked Mackerel Pate

Ingredients:

- 8 oz (225g) smoked mackerel fillets, skin removed
- 4 oz (115g) cream cheese, softened
- 2 tablespoons mayonnaise
- 1 tablespoon fresh lemon juice
- 1 tablespoon chopped fresh dill (optional)
- Salt and pepper, to taste
- Crackers, bread, or vegetable sticks, for serving

Instructions:

1. Prepare the mackerel: Flake the smoked mackerel fillets into a bowl, removing any skin and bones.
2. Mix the ingredients: Add the softened cream cheese, mayonnaise, fresh lemon juice, and chopped fresh dill (if using) to the bowl with the flaked mackerel. Season with salt and pepper, to taste.
3. Combine: Use a fork or spoon to mix all the ingredients together until well combined and creamy. Taste and adjust the seasoning, if needed.
4. Chill: Cover the bowl with plastic wrap and refrigerate the mackerel pâté for at least 30 minutes to allow the flavors to meld and the mixture to firm up slightly.
5. Serve: Once chilled, transfer the smoked mackerel pâté to a serving dish. Serve with crackers, bread, or vegetable sticks for dipping.
6. Garnish: Garnish the pâté with additional chopped fresh dill or a slice of lemon, if desired, for a decorative touch.
7. Enjoy: Enjoy your homemade smoked mackerel pâté as an appetizer, snack, or party dip. It's perfect for entertaining or enjoying with family and friends!

This smoked mackerel pâté is creamy, flavorful, and packed with protein and omega-3 fatty acids from the mackerel. It's a versatile dish that's sure to be a hit at any gathering or occasion. Enjoy making and savoring this delicious pâté!

Clapshot

Ingredients:

- 2 large potatoes, peeled and diced
- 2 large swedes (rutabagas), peeled and diced
- 4 tablespoons butter
- Salt and pepper, to taste
- Chopped fresh parsley, for garnish (optional)

Instructions:

1. Cook the vegetables: Place the diced potatoes and swedes in a large pot and cover them with cold water. Bring the water to a boil over high heat, then reduce the heat to medium and simmer the vegetables until they are tender, about 15-20 minutes.
2. Drain the vegetables: Once the potatoes and swedes are cooked through, drain them well in a colander.
3. Mash the vegetables: Return the drained potatoes and swedes to the pot. Add the butter to the pot and mash the vegetables with a potato masher until smooth and creamy. Alternatively, you can use a potato ricer for a finer texture.
4. Season: Season the clapshot with salt and pepper, to taste. Adjust the seasoning as needed.
5. Serve: Transfer the clapshot to a serving dish and garnish with chopped fresh parsley, if desired. Serve hot as a side dish alongside roasted meats, sausages, or other Scottish dishes.

Clapshot is a comforting and hearty dish that pairs well with a variety of mains. Its creamy texture and earthy flavor make it a beloved side dish in Scottish cuisine. Enjoy making and savoring this simple and delicious recipe!

Scotch Beef Wellington

Ingredients:

- 1 ½ lb (about 700g) beef fillet, trimmed
- Salt and pepper, to taste
- 2 tablespoons olive oil
- 2 tablespoons Dijon mustard
- 8 oz (225g) mushrooms, finely chopped
- 2 cloves garlic, minced
- 2 tablespoons butter
- 2 tablespoons chopped fresh thyme
- 1 sheet of puff pastry, thawed if frozen
- 4 slices of Parma ham or prosciutto
- 1 egg, beaten (for egg wash)

Instructions:

1. Preheat the oven: Preheat your oven to 400°F (200°C).
2. Prepare the beef: Season the beef fillet generously with salt and pepper. Heat the olive oil in a large skillet over high heat. Sear the beef fillet on all sides until browned, about 1-2 minutes per side. Remove from heat and let it cool slightly.
3. Brush with mustard: Brush the seared beef fillet with Dijon mustard all over. This will help the mushroom duxelles stick to the beef.
4. Make the mushroom duxelles: In the same skillet, melt the butter over medium heat. Add the chopped mushrooms and minced garlic to the skillet. Cook, stirring occasionally, until the mushrooms release their moisture and turn golden brown, about 8-10 minutes. Stir in the chopped fresh thyme and season with salt and pepper to taste. Remove from heat and let it cool slightly.
5. Assemble the Wellington: Lay out a large sheet of plastic wrap on a clean surface. Arrange the slices of Parma ham or prosciutto on the plastic wrap, overlapping them slightly to form a large rectangle. Spread the mushroom duxelles evenly over the ham.
6. Place the seared beef fillet in the center of the mushroom-covered ham. Using the plastic wrap to help you, carefully roll the ham and mushroom mixture around the beef fillet to encase it completely. Twist the ends of the plastic wrap to tighten the bundle. Chill the wrapped beef fillet in the refrigerator for 15-20 minutes to firm up.

7. Roll out the puff pastry: On a lightly floured surface, roll out the puff pastry into a large rectangle, large enough to completely encase the beef fillet.
8. Wrap the beef: Unwrap the chilled beef fillet from the plastic wrap and place it in the center of the puff pastry. Carefully fold the pastry over the beef, pressing the edges to seal. Trim any excess pastry and crimp the edges with a fork to secure. Brush the pastry with beaten egg for a golden finish.
9. Bake the Wellington: Transfer the wrapped beef fillet to a baking sheet lined with parchment paper. Bake in the preheated oven for 25-30 minutes, or until the pastry is golden brown and crispy, and the beef reaches your desired level of doneness. For medium-rare, the internal temperature should register 130-135°F (55-57°C) on a meat thermometer.
10. Rest and serve: Once baked, remove the Beef Wellington from the oven and let it rest for a few minutes before slicing. Slice into thick slices and serve immediately.

Scotch Beef Wellington is a show-stopping dish that's perfect for special occasions or a gourmet dinner at home. Enjoy the tender beef, savory mushroom duxelles, and flaky puff pastry in every bite!

Scottish Cheese Platter

Selection of Cheeses:

1. Isle of Mull Cheddar: A tangy and crumbly cheddar cheese with a distinctive flavor, made on the Isle of Mull using traditional methods.
2. Crowdie: A soft and creamy Scottish cheese made from skimmed cow's milk. It has a mild flavor and a slightly grainy texture.
3. Blue Murder: A bold and creamy blue cheese with a rich, tangy flavor. It is made from cow's milk and aged to develop its distinctive blue veining.
4. Strathdon Blue: Another Scottish blue cheese with a creamy texture and a milder flavor profile compared to Blue Murder. It pairs well with fruit and nuts.
5. Caboc: A traditional Scottish cream cheese shaped into a log and rolled in oats. It has a smooth and buttery texture with a subtle tanginess.

Accompaniments:

1. Oatcakes: Traditional Scottish oatcakes made from oats, flour, and butter. They have a crumbly texture and a slightly nutty flavor, making them the perfect vehicle for cheese.
2. Scottish Honey: A drizzle of Scottish honey adds a touch of sweetness that pairs beautifully with the savory cheeses.
3. Fresh Fruits: Serve a selection of fresh fruits such as apples, pears, and grapes to complement the richness of the cheeses.
4. Chutney or Relish: A tangy chutney or relish adds a burst of flavor and complexity to the cheese platter. Opt for a Scottish variety such as apple and thistle chutney.
5. Nuts: Toasted nuts such as almonds or walnuts add crunch and texture to the platter. They also complement the creamy cheeses.
6. Whisky: Finish off the platter with a glass of Scotch whisky for an authentic Scottish experience. Choose a whisky with smoky or peaty notes to complement the robust flavors of the cheeses.

Assembly:

Arrange the cheeses on a large platter, leaving space between each cheese for accompaniments. Place small bowls or ramekins of chutney, honey, and nuts around the cheeses. Fill in the remaining space with oatcakes and fresh fruits. Serve with glasses of whisky on the side.

Creating a Scottish cheese platter is a wonderful way to celebrate the flavors and traditions of Scotland. Enjoy exploring the rich variety of cheeses and accompaniments, and savoring them with friends and family.

Scottish Gin and Tonic Cake

Ingredients:

- 1 3/4 cups (220g) all-purpose flour
- 2 teaspoons baking powder
- 1/2 teaspoon salt
- 1 cup (200g) granulated sugar
- Zest of 1 lemon
- 1/2 cup (120ml) vegetable oil
- 3 large eggs
- 1/4 cup (60ml) gin
- 1/4 cup (60ml) tonic water
- 1 teaspoon vanilla extract

For the Gin and Tonic Glaze:

- 1/4 cup (60ml) gin
- 1/4 cup (60ml) tonic water
- 1/2 cup (100g) granulated sugar

For the Lemon Glaze:

- 1 cup (120g) powdered sugar
- 2-3 tablespoons lemon juice

Instructions:

1. Preheat the oven: Preheat your oven to 350°F (175°C). Grease and flour a 9-inch (23cm) bundt cake pan.
2. Mix dry ingredients: In a mixing bowl, whisk together the flour, baking powder, and salt until well combined.
3. Prepare wet ingredients: In a separate mixing bowl, combine the granulated sugar and lemon zest. Rub the zest into the sugar with your fingers until fragrant. Add the vegetable oil, eggs, gin, tonic water, and vanilla extract to the sugar mixture. Whisk until smooth and well combined.

4. Combine wet and dry ingredients: Gradually add the dry ingredients to the wet ingredients, mixing until just combined. Be careful not to overmix.
5. Bake: Pour the batter into the prepared bundt pan and smooth the top with a spatula. Bake in the preheated oven for 35-40 minutes, or until a toothpick inserted into the center of the cake comes out clean.
6. Make the Gin and Tonic Glaze: While the cake is baking, prepare the gin and tonic glaze. In a small saucepan, combine the gin, tonic water, and granulated sugar. Heat over medium heat, stirring constantly, until the sugar has dissolved and the mixture has thickened slightly, about 5 minutes. Remove from heat and let cool slightly.
7. Remove the cake: Once the cake is done baking, remove it from the oven and let it cool in the pan for 10 minutes. Then, invert the cake onto a wire rack set over a baking sheet.
8. Glaze the cake: While the cake is still warm, brush the gin and tonic glaze over the surface of the cake, allowing it to soak in. Let the cake cool completely.
9. Make the Lemon Glaze: In a small bowl, whisk together the powdered sugar and lemon juice until smooth. Drizzle the lemon glaze over the cooled cake.
10. Serve: Slice and serve the Scottish Gin and Tonic Cake, garnished with lemon zest or slices, if desired. Enjoy with a cup of tea or coffee, or even a gin and tonic!

This Scottish Gin and Tonic Cake is a unique and flavorful dessert that's perfect for special occasions or afternoon tea. The combination of gin, tonic water, and lemon creates a refreshing and zesty flavor that's sure to impress. Enjoy making and savoring this delicious cake!

Scottish Ale and Beef Stew

Ingredients:

- 2 lbs (about 900g) beef stew meat, cut into bite-sized pieces
- Salt and pepper, to taste
- 2 tablespoons vegetable oil
- 2 onions, chopped
- 2 carrots, diced
- 2 celery stalks, diced
- 2 cloves garlic, minced
- 2 tablespoons tomato paste
- 2 tablespoons all-purpose flour
- 2 cups (480ml) Scottish ale or any dark ale
- 2 cups (480ml) beef broth
- 2 bay leaves
- 1 teaspoon dried thyme
- 1 teaspoon dried rosemary
- 4 potatoes, peeled and diced
- Chopped fresh parsley, for garnish (optional)

Instructions:

1. Season the beef: Season the beef stew meat generously with salt and pepper.
2. Brown the beef: Heat the vegetable oil in a large pot or Dutch oven over medium-high heat. Add the seasoned beef to the pot in batches and cook until browned on all sides. Remove the beef from the pot and set aside.
3. Cook the vegetables: In the same pot, add the chopped onions, diced carrots, and diced celery. Cook, stirring occasionally, until the vegetables are softened, about 5-7 minutes. Add the minced garlic and cook for an additional minute.
4. Add the tomato paste and flour: Stir in the tomato paste and all-purpose flour, and cook for 1-2 minutes, until the flour is lightly browned and the tomato paste is fragrant.
5. Deglaze the pot: Pour in the Scottish ale, using a wooden spoon to scrape up any browned bits from the bottom of the pot. Allow the ale to come to a simmer and cook for a few minutes to reduce slightly.

6. Add the beef broth and seasonings: Stir in the beef broth, bay leaves, dried thyme, and dried rosemary. Return the browned beef to the pot and bring the mixture to a simmer. Cover and cook for 1-2 hours, or until the beef is tender.
7. Add the potatoes: Once the beef is tender, add the diced potatoes to the pot. Cover and continue to simmer for an additional 30-45 minutes, or until the potatoes are cooked through and the stew has thickened.
8. Adjust seasoning and serve: Taste the stew and adjust the seasoning with salt and pepper, if needed. Remove the bay leaves before serving. Garnish with chopped fresh parsley, if desired.
9. Serve: Ladle the Scottish ale and beef stew into bowls and serve hot, accompanied by crusty bread or your favorite side dishes.

This Scottish ale and beef stew is rich, hearty, and full of comforting flavors. Enjoy making and savoring it on a cozy evening at home!

Scottish Butter Tablet

Ingredients:

- 2 cups (400g) granulated sugar
- 1 cup (240ml) whole milk
- 1 cup (225g) unsalted butter, plus extra for greasing
- 1 can (397g) sweetened condensed milk
- Pinch of salt

Instructions:

1. Prepare the pan: Grease a shallow baking dish or tray with butter. Set aside.
2. Combine ingredients: In a large, heavy-bottomed saucepan, combine the granulated sugar, whole milk, unsalted butter, sweetened condensed milk, and a pinch of salt.
3. Cook: Place the saucepan over medium heat and stir the mixture constantly until the sugar has dissolved and the butter has melted. Once the mixture comes to a boil, reduce the heat to low and simmer gently, stirring frequently, for about 25-30 minutes. Be careful as the mixture will be very hot.
4. Test for readiness: To test if the tablet mixture is ready, drop a small amount into a bowl of cold water. If it forms a soft ball when rolled between your fingers, it's ready.
5. Beat the mixture: Remove the saucepan from the heat and beat the mixture vigorously with a wooden spoon for about 5-10 minutes, or until it starts to thicken and lose its glossiness. This process helps to create the crumbly texture of the tablet.
6. Pour into the pan: Quickly pour the mixture into the prepared baking dish or tray and smooth the top with a spatula.
7. Cool and cut: Let the tablet cool completely at room temperature for several hours, or until set. Once set, use a sharp knife to cut the tablet into squares or rectangles.
8. Serve: Serve the Scottish Butter Tablet as a sweet treat with tea or coffee, or package it up in decorative boxes to give as gifts.

Store any leftover tablet in an airtight container at room temperature for up to two weeks.

This Scottish Butter Tablet recipe yields a deliciously sweet and crumbly treat that's perfect for indulging in on special occasions or sharing with friends and family. Enjoy making and savoring this traditional Scottish confectionery!

www.ingramcontent.com/pod-product-compliance
Lightning Source LLC
LaVergne TN
LVHW062048070526
838201LV00080B/2202